one wild ride

the life of skateboarding superstar

Tony Hawk

by mark stewart

TWENTY-FIRST CENTURY BOOKS
BROOKFIELD, CONNECTICUT

TFCB

Twenty-First Century Books

Produced by
Bittersweet Publishing
John Sammis, President
and
Team Stewart, Inc.
Researched and edited by Mike Kennedy

Design and Electronic Page Makeup by
Jaffe Enterprises
Ron Jaffe

All photos courtesy J. Grant Brittain except the following:
AP/ Wide World Photos, Inc. — Pages 6, 9, 10, 12, 25, 37, 39
Birdhouse Skateboards © 2001 (Web site) — Page 44
Tony Hawk, Inc. © 2001 (Web site) — Page 58
The following images are from the collection of Team Stewart:
Sports Illustrated for Kids/TIME Inc. © 2000 — Page 11
National Fluid Milk Processor Board © 1999 — Page 31
Sports Illustrated for Kids/TIME Inc. © 1997 — Page 41
Sports Illustrated for Kids/TIME Inc. © 2001 — Page 52
Activision © 1999 — Page 55
Sports Illustrated for Kids/TIME Inc. © 2001 — Page 59

Printed in Hong Kong

Published by Twenty-First Century Books
A Division of The Millbrook Press, Inc.
2 Old New Milford Road
Brookfield, Connecticut   06804

www.millbrookpress.com

Library of Congress Cataloging-in-Publication Data

Stewart, Mark.
   One wild ride : the life of skateboarding superstar Tony Hawk / by Mark Stewart.
      p. cm.
Includes index.
Summary: A biography of the professional skateboarder, Tony Hawk, focusing on his inventive
moves, competitions, fatherhood, and business enterprises.
   ISBN 0-7613-2666-9 (lib. bdg.)   ISBN 0-7613-1689-2 (pbk.)
   1. Hawk, Tony—Juvenile literature. 2. Skateboarders—United States—Biography—Juvenile
literature. [1. Hawk, Tony. 2. Skateboarders.] I. Title: Life of skateboarding superstar Tony
Hawk. II. Title.
   GV859.813.H39 S74 2002
   796.22'092—dc21
                                                                           2001008031

1 3 5 7 9 10 8 6 4 2

contents

chapter 1

nothing short of perfect

"I was a hyper, rail-thin geek on a sugar buzz."
TONY HAWK

Frank and Nancy Hawk were not planning to have any more kids. In the autumn of 1967, both were in their 40s, with two daughters in college and a son in the eighth grade. Like most people their age, the Hawks were starting to plan their "golden" years, when the kids were grown and they had some time to themselves. Nancy was attending night school to get an advanced degree in education. Frank, who as a young man had flown bombers in World War II and the Korean War, was now in a less hazardous occupation: He sold washing machines and refrigerators in San Diego, California. When Nancy's

Like father like son.
**Tony feels most at home when he is in midair,
defying the pull of gravity. His dad, a former pilot, felt the same way.**

5

Look, Mom, no hands!
When skateboarding first took off in the early 1960s, it was an earthbound fad. The sport has changed quite a bit since then.

doctor informed her she was pregnant, the family was in shock. The Hawks knew their lives would change with the arrival of their fourth child. But not in a million years could they have imagined how much.

Tony Hawk was born on May 12, 1968. He grew up in a loving home. Tony's parents indulged and supported their children's interests and talents. His oldest sister, Lenore, had an ear for languages and would one day become a teacher. His other sister, Pat, was a gifted singer and artist. His older brother, Steve, was a writer and a surfing nut. The Hawk house was always busy, always noisy, and always filled with laughter. The family had a quirky sense of humor, and they loved having a little kid around.

As the baby of the family, Tony soon learned he could get away with things his older siblings never would have dreamed of. He tried anything that popped into his little head; rarely was he scolded—even when he did something dangerous. "Instead of the terrible twos, I was the terrible youth," Tony recalls. "I think my mom summed it up best when she said I was *challenging*."

Tony also developed an intense desire to win. When he lost, he sometimes threw temper tantrums. Tony's parents thought it might be a good idea to point him toward sports like swimming, where the focus was as much on technical improvement as on beating opponents. Tony was a good swimmer, but spent as much time under the water as he did on top of it. He liked to see how far he could swim without coming up for air, pushing himself right to the edge of drowning. When Tony was six, his mother brought him to an Olympic-size swimming pool. "He decided that he had to swim the length of it without a breath," Nancy Hawk recalls. "And then he was so frustrated when he didn't do it. He was so hard on himself and expected himself to do so many things."

Two sides to Tony.
It took him years before he learned how to relax and take life less seriously.

In school, Tony looked to push the limits, too. He picked up on new ideas faster than his classmates, and was often bored with the slow pace of class. In second grade, he decided he would move things along himself by holding "class" after the final bell had rung. Tony and his neighborhood friends would gather at his house, where he would drill them in math. Soon it was obvious that he was going too fast for the other children. Tony was placed in special advanced classes. He liked learning at an accelerated rate, but was miserable being separated from children his own age. In the end, he decided he would rather go back to his classroom and just "hang."

> ## check it out...
> Tony's sister Pat had a successful musical career. She sang back-up for the Righteous Brothers, John Denver, and Michael Bolton.

The summer after Tony turned eight years old, the Hawks moved to Terrasanta, California. He joined the local youth leagues in basketball and baseball. Frank Hawk, who loved watching Tony compete, coached his Little League team. He was disappointed that Tony did not have the baseball skills some other boys did, but proud that no one out-hustled or outworked his son.

What concerned him, however, was that Tony seemed to be a "perfectionist"—someone who cannot tolerate anything less than a flawless performance. In some sports this is good. In sports like baseball and basketball, where players make outs and miss shots more often than not, it can be crippling. Whenever Tony threw a bad pass or made an error, he sulked. He hated the fact that he had let his teammates down. One day, after he struck out in a baseball game, he ran from the field and squeezed himself into a cave. Frank did not know what to do— Tony obviously needed the physical and mental challenges of sports,

Dude, sign my cap!
When Tony was a kid, there were no skateboarding pros he could look up to. Today, he is The Man.

but not if sports made him miserable.

The answer to this dilemma was buried in the garage all along. Like most kids in the 1960s, Tony's brother, Steve, had tried skateboarding. The boards back then were nothing like they are today. They were clumsy, heavy chunks of wood attached to metal roller-skate wheels. Steve lost interest in his skateboard and threw it in a box. One day, when Steve was home on a visit from college, he pulled out the old board. Tony's eyes lit up. "Steve gave me his old skateboard and taught me how to cruise on the street," Tony says, matter-of-factly. He forgets to mention that after a few tentative moments, he was rolling down the driveway as if he were *born* to be on that board. Tony was a natural.

2 making his bones

"I was the skinny kid with a squeaky voice who skated endlessly and looked ridiculous."

TONY HAWK

Steve Hawk showed his little brother classic moves like the Ollie and Rock-n-Roll, which he quickly mastered. Then Tony began thinking up ones of his own. He and his friends would practice endlessly in driveways and cul-de-sacs. Whenever they could get a ride, they would visit the Oasis Skatepark in San Diego, a 15-minute drive from their neighborhood.

Grab some pavement.
The tricks of the trade were pretty basic when Tony got his first board. But all over California, kids were starting to push the limits of the sport.

Rookie Card.
Tony, age 9, is pictured on one of his most in-demand trading cards.

TONY HAWK

Sports Illustrated KiDS

Age 9

SKATEBOARDER ◆ CARLSBAD, CALIFORNIA

Skateboarding was different than the other sports Tony had tried. When he failed to do a trick, he did not get angry or discouraged. Instead, he got right back on the board and tried it again. And again. And again. It was the ideal outlet for his personality—his love of "pushing the limits" and his relentless quest for perfection. Tony's family watched as the youngest Hawk went through a stunning metamorphosis. "When he started getting good at skating it changed his personality," recalls Steve. "Finally he was doing something that he was satisfied with. He became a different guy; he was calm, he started thinking about other people, and became more generous."

Tony's family definitely wanted to encourage him to explore this sport some more. His parents bought him a modern skateboard with a flexible, lightweight deck and pavement-gripping polyurethane wheels. Tony calls it his first "real" board. Frank built him a small ramp in the driveway, while Nancy and Steve took turns driving him to Oasis.

Soon Tony was obsessed with skateboarding. He got a paper route in the mornings to earn money for equipment, and went to the skatepark almost every afternoon. He no longer skated with his friends—they were not serious enough for him. The kids he met at Oasis *were* into skateboarding, yet Tony mostly kept to himself. He was too focused on improving his technique and trying to do things no one else was doing.

In 1979, Tony came across a copy of *Skateboarder*, a new magazine dedicated to his fast-growing sport. He was astonished by the publication's awesome photos, and fascinated by the equipment reviews, news, and skater profiles contained in its pages. Tony realized that he was not alone in his obsession; there were boys just like him all over the country and around the world. He was not sure if you could make a living at skateboarding, but he knew that—somehow, some way—this was what he wanted to do when he grew up.

Although Tony did not realize it, skateboarding at this time was starting to have an image problem. More and more, skateboarders thought of themselves as rebels. Many moved from the controlled environment of skateparks and thumbed their noses at society by doing dangerous stunts in public places. Some even adopted the severe dress and hairstyles of punk musicians. The angrier adults got, the more the skateboarders liked it. Tony was not looking

"It's exciting to be upside down in the air and have the feeling I know where I'm at."
TONY HAWK

for trouble—he had simply fallen in love with the sport. He was only interested in finding new ways to improve and compete. And although he tried as many dangerous stunts as other skateboarders, the risk was

Thin mint.
Tony's long, gangly body led him to develop his own set of original moves.

not what interested him. "Skating isn't about danger," Tony says. "It's about doing things that are really progressive and athletic."

Tony's first appearance in official competition came at Oasis when he was 11 years old. The night before the meet he was so nervous he could barely sleep. On the way to the park that morning, he went through his run over and over again in his head. When it came time to skate, however, Tony froze up. Unable to relax, he fell on his easiest tricks and got awful marks from the judges. As soon as he finished, he asked his parents to drive him home. To this day he does not know where he finished.

The disaster at Oasis only made Tony work harder. He continued to devote all his free time to skateboarding. He thought about what had

C'mon Dad!
Frank Hawk was never far from Tony early in his career.

made him so nervous in competition and realized that deep down he did not yet believe in himself. Tony vowed not to enter another meet until he was totally self-confident, until he could perform doubt-free. "When I skate, I never go halfway," he says today. "If I don't do my best, it eats at me. It kills me inside."

Tony also knew that he had to alter his style. Tall and gangly for his age, he weighed less and had a different center of gravity than most other skaters. The tricks they performed were aggressive "power" moves. Tony could not generate this kind of power, so he began thinking up tricks that worked for *his* body. With his intelligence, imagination, and dedication it was not long before Tony could do things on a skateboard that no one had ever seen before. His confidence and creativity began to impress judges, and his scores in competition climbed higher and higher. Tony learned an important lesson: As he puts it, "There's not a set of rules and a certain way you have to skate to be a skater."

Frank Hawk sensed that his son was doing something special. But he also saw that skateboarding was losing popularity. He worried that one day Tony might not have anywhere to demonstrate his breathtaking moves. Indeed, the number of meets in southern California was already on the decline. Frank began asking local businesses to help finance an official skateboarding league. Toward the end of 1980, the California Amateur Skateboard League (CASL) was born. It hosted competitions throughout the region and played a key role in keeping the sport alive. "I always said I was doing it for other kids," Tony's father once said, "but subconsciously, I was doing it for Tony."

Frank helped his son in other ways. Prior to one meet, he invited Denise Barter to stay in the family's guest room for a few days. Barter worked for Dogtown, a well-known skateboarding company in northern California. While visiting with the Hawks, she got to watch Tony practice and perform. She was impressed with his approach, and believed that he was the kind of skater who might lift their sport out of the doldrums. Barter asked Tony if he would like to be sponsored by Dogtown. The company would supply him with all the boards and equipment he needed if he promised to promote Dogtown wherever he skated.

check it out...

When Tony was 11, he fell while practicing alone at a skatepark. He was found unconscious and rushed to the hospital. Initially, doctors thought he might be an abused child. "The doctors were suspicious because of all the bruises and scabs I had—but I explained it," says Tony, adding, "My dad bought me a helmet after that."

Tony could hardly believe his ears. He thought for about one second before saying *yes*.

In addition to all the cool stuff Tony got from Dogtown, the company paid for him to enter more important contests. With state-of-the-art equipment and better competition, he quickly raised the level of his performance. He also began to catch the eye of some important skate-

Rim shot.
Skateboarding legend Stacy Peralta.

boarding people. One was Stacy Peralta, a legendary skater who co-owned Powell-Peralta, one of the biggest names in the business. Peralta thought Tony had the makings of a world-class skateboarder. He also knew that Dogtown—like many small companies in the sport—was struggling to survive. Tony had been skating for Dogtown less than a year when the bad news came: The company was going out of business. A short time later, Peralta called to ask if Tony would be interested in joining his team of skaters, known throughout the sport as the "Bones Brigade."

What an honor this was! He would be touring with some of the country's top skaters, including well-known professionals Rodney Mullen, Steve Caballero, and Mike McGill. Hundreds of spectators came to watch this trio and get their autographs wherever they appeared. "When I was growing up, I saw Steve Caballero in a magazine," Tony remembers. "He was like thirteen and doing four-foot air, which was as big as you could go at the time. I really got inspired and thought, *Wow, he's not much older than me, and he's launching.*"

Starting in the summer of 1981, Tony would be riding with Steve.

I'm not worthy!

Tony worshiped Steve Caballero when he joined the Bones Brigade tour in 1981. Later, Steve credited Tony with taking the sport to a whole new level.

3 chapter

hanging in there

"It's great that people realize that what we do is athletic, and not just an outlaw activity."

TONY HAWK

Blowing away the top amateurs in southern California had been getting a bit boring for Tony, so the move to Powell-Peralta seemed like the right move at the right time. It would not be an *easy* move, however. That summer, the Bones Brigade traveled all over the country. At every stop Tony encountered skaters who were far more advanced than he was—not to mention the fact that his teammates were leaving him in the dust, too. At his first major event, in Florida, Tony got totally smoked by the competition. It was embarrassing.

The good news was that Tony learned a lot during the summer of 1981, and made steady improvement. He also noticed other top skaters attempting to copy *his* tricks. It was flattering to see them try his moves, and a little funny to see the results. Usually, they landed in a crumpled heap.

More good news came that fall. The Hawk family was moving north to Cardiff. The Oasis Skatepark had fallen out of favor with skaters, and the owners had let it get rundown. Tony's new home in Cardiff was just a few minutes from the Del Mar Surf and Turf, a first-rate skatepark that attracted the hottest riders in the area.

Tony was ready for the change of scenery for another reason: At his old school, skateboarders were considered outcasts, and he was constantly teased. In Cardiff, he hoped to make a fresh start. Unfortunately, things went from bad to worse. Tony enrolled at San Dieguito High School, where the upperclassmen made fun of the way he dressed and the way he looked. Even worse, the school administration banned skateboards altogether. "In my high school, there

Boarding house.
Young Tony stirs up the crowd on his home turf in Del Mar.

Open Mike.
Mike McGill, a teammate on the Bones Brigade, encouraged Tony to try new stunts.

were only two other skaters," says Tony. "It definitely wasn't considered cool."

Tony's only escape was the Surf and Turf, where he practiced nonstop after school. Toward the end of his freshman year at San Dieguito, he faced some tough decisions. Tony was already spending almost every minute of his free time skateboarding, and felt he should be earning money for it—just the way other kids get paid to do after-school jobs. He told his parents he wanted to become a professional skateboarder. They told him to go for it. So did Stacy Peralta, who believed Tony's career was about to take off.

Tony also had to decide what to do about school. The big kids were still picking on him, and it was getting to the point where he could not take it anymore. Tony visited nearby Torrey Pines High School. From the moment he set foot on campus, he sensed that this was a place where he would feel welcome. The students seemed friendlier and more open-minded. The social structure was not as rigid. And best of all, the principal had done a little surfing and skateboarding himself. He had even heard of Tony before! Over the summer, the Hawks arranged for their son to transfer.

This was the summer during which Tony joined the professional skateboarding ranks. He placed third in his first pro event, then won his second meet. He finished sixth in his third competition. Most 14-year-olds would have been thrilled with those results. However, Tony worried that skateboarding was a dying sport. His dream was to one day support himself as a professional, yet there was little enthusiasm for pro skateboarding and almost no prize money available.

Once again, Frank Hawk stepped in. In 1983, he started the National Skateboarding Association (NSA). It marked the first time in the sport's history that the top skaters and top skateboard companies unified to form a pro league. The NSA focused all the strengths of the sport in one place while minimizing its weaknesses. Tony, who blossomed during his carefree year at Torrey Pines, became a superstar. He won the NSA's first event, and consistently outscored the competition all summer.

The only problem was that Tony's father was the NSA's president. Rival skaters, tired of watching Tony outperform them, began to whisper that the meets were "fixed." They claimed that, since the judges were hired by Frank, they gave special consideration to his son. Instead of being proud of his accomplishments, Tony felt a little guilty. "Tony was

check it out...

Falling is part of skateboarding. So are the bumps, bruises, and occasional broken bones that come with it. In Tony's case, his worst falls have occurred during his simplest tricks. "The times you can get hurt the most in skating are when you're doing something very basic," he says. Tony cautions all riders to pay extra attention when they are practicing their easiest moves.

embarrassed winning contests organized by my father, scored by judges who answered to my father," confirms his brother, Steve.

Some thought Tony's dad should quit. But they knew the NSA would fold without his leadership. It was a complicated time. Frank decided to speak out. He let it be known that yes, like any other father, he wanted his child to do well. But anyone who believed that he would give Tony an unfair advantage obviously did not know him very well. In time, the others saw how much integrity Frank Hawk had, and the rumors stopped.

That summer, Tony took a break from NSA competition and went back on the road with the Bones Brigade. He traveled to Australia, Europe, Canada, and across the U.S., competing in contests and performing technical demonstrations. Tony found that his graceful midair moves were catching on with fans, and with judges, too. They were getting bored with the power moves of the older skaters, and more interested in the subtle tricks Tony was doing. At times, he and his board seemed to hang suspended in the air, as if he were breaking the grip of gravity. This was good for the sport—it meant it was "evolving."

And obviously, it was good for Tony. He made some money that summer, and won his first event outside of California, in St. Petersburg, Florida. Also, sales of the Powell-Peralta skateboards and equipment he endorsed were beginning to climb. Tony returned to California in time to enter the NSA's final event, and finished fourth. With his first-place finishes at the beginning of the year, he had accumulated enough points to end the season as his sport's first official national champion.

Northern exposure.
Tony hit the road during the summer of 1983, including this midair stop in Vancouver, Canada.

hanging is there

4 chapter

wheels of fortune

"Tony is the best skater around."

STEVE CABALLERO

Tony's second year at Torrey Pines High was terrific. He did well in class, made a couple of friends, and no one seemed to know or care that he was the country's top skateboarder. In 1984, Tony skated in a bunch of NSA events and also went on tour again with the Bones Brigade. The fans all seemed to know him this time around, and cheered loudly when he performed. A tape called the *Bones Brigade Video Show* was selling briskly, and this added to his fame. When Tony's tricks were shown in slow motion, people could

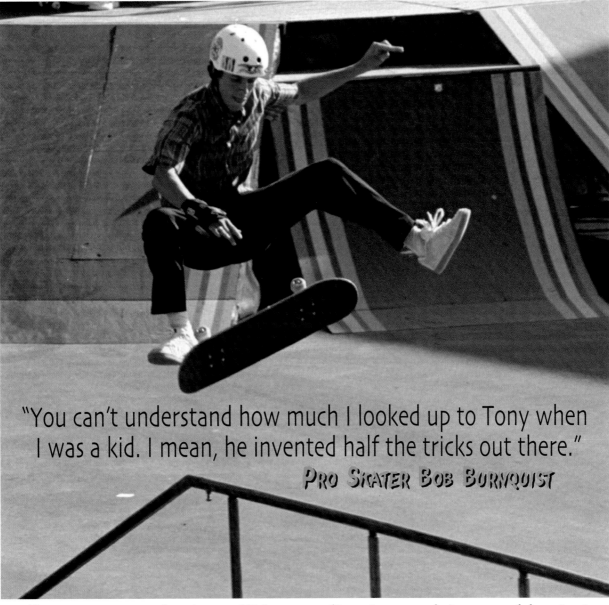

"You can't understand how much I looked up to Tony when I was a kid. I mean, he invented half the tricks out there."

PRO SKATER BOB BURNQUIST

really appreciate the incredible coordination and impeccable timing required to complete them. More important, the crowd seemed much larger than the year before. Maybe, Tony thought, his sport was on the rebound.

AR SKATE RANCH

Tall story.
As Tony kept growing, he kept inventing tricks that would take advantage of his high center of gravity.

When autumn came and school began, things got even better for Tony. He won his second NSA championship in September, and in October met his future wife, Cindy Dunbar. Tony was also putting some money in the bank. For the first time, it looked as if he might make a decent living from skateboarding. The year ended on a sad note, however, when Frank Hawk suffered a heart attack. Luckily, Tony was with his father at the time and immediately dialed 911. While they waited for help to arrive, Tony let his father know how much he appreciated him. "In the minutes before the ambulance arrived, when he was feeling helpless, he really opened up to my dad," confirms Steve

Launch break.
Frank Hawk needed little time before he bounced back from his heart attack. Meanwhile, Tony was becoming the biggest name in skateboarding.

Hawk. "He told him how much he loved him. How he was the greatest father. How he appreciated everything he had done."

Those who knew Tony's dad found it hard to believe that a bad heart would slow him down. And they were right. He survived the attack and by the following spring had resumed his hectic schedule. With the Hawks in charge, the NSA had really taken flight. By this time NSA events were being held all over the country, and Tony was the sport's biggest drawing card. He seemed to come up with something new for almost every big competition, and he was in constant demand. In 1985, he completed taping of Stacy Peralta's *Future Primitive*, a sequel to the first Bones Brigade video.

Tony also spent five weeks as an instructor at a skateboarding camp in Sweden. He was amazed to see how popular the sport was on the other side of the Atlantic Ocean. While at the camp, he kept a daily journal. Tony was trying to invent a new grab, where he reached behind his back with his trailing hand and grasped the board between his sneakers. One of the campers peeked at his account of the day, and asked if *stale fish* was the weird backward grab he was working on. Tony had actually been describing the awful meal that was being served. But since he had not named this trick yet, he said *yes*. Nearly 20 years later, the Stalefish remains one of the standard skateboarding moves!

That fall, Tony won the last two NSA events, in Arkansas and Texas, to earn his third national championship. When the video *Future Primitive* was released, letters from enthusiastic admirers began pouring in. Tony read each one. People were totally turned on by his unique style and spirit. They asked why no one else skated the way he did. They wanted to know what new tricks he was working on. For Tony, who had secretly been self-conscious about his approach to skateboarding, the compliments meant as much as the money he was now making. Between prizes, endorsement contracts, and appearance fees, he had made more than $100,000 in 1985. Not bad for a 17-year-old!

The only regrets Tony had about 1985 concerned his grades. He was spending so much time on his career that his schoolwork had begun to suffer. Instead of As and Bs, he got mostly Cs in the fall semester of his senior year at Torrey Pines. Luckily, he had done well enough in past years to guarantee that he would graduate on time, in June of 1986. That spring, his sister Patricia suggested that he take advantage of the booming real-estate market in California and invest his skateboard earnings in a house. Tony followed her advice and bought a little home in Carlsbad, a few exits up the freeway from where his parents lived.

check it out...

Not all of Tony's video appearances make his personal "greatest hits." Often, he appears in the "slam" section, which shows riders messing up. On one tape he is featured sliding down the ramp after he fell and was knocked out.

Gnaw on this!
The Stalefish, now a standard skating move, was a Hawk original.

As remarkable as it was for a high school student to purchase his own home, perhaps the most amazing thing to happen in Tony's life was his sudden popularity. Classmates who never bothered to say hello to him now hung on his every word. When he invited a few friends to his house for a party, dozens of people would show up. Tony had never wanted to be a celebrity, and this was one of the reasons —you never know whether people like you for who you are or because you are famous.

This was just a taste of things to come. Until Tony began to understand his fame and use it wisely, others would try to use his fame for their own purposes. This became clear later in the year when he was talked into doing a small part in a movie called *Thrashin'*. The producers

Air head.
It took a while for Tony to figure out that popularity and fame aren't always what they seem to be.

set up a two-day shoot at the Surf and Turf, and Tony agreed to appear mainly because he thought it would be fun to return to his "roots." When the movie was released, he realized he had been tricked. Tony's image was being used to promote *Thrashin'* all over California, including on a gigantic billboard in Los Angeles. Although he appeared in the film for a very short amount of time, from the publicity it looked like he was the star. Tony's fans were disappointed when they realized he was only on-screen for a few brief moments.

Despite the pitfalls of fame, Tony had a great 1986 season. He worked with Stacy Peralta again, this time on a video called *The Search for Animal Chin*. He also found time to compete on the NSA circuit, capturing his fourth national title in a row. Tony was dominating his sport, but in a "good" way. Because he hardly ever fell, rival skaters were forced to do something extraordinary in order to beat him. This almost always resulted in spectacular wipeouts, but once or twice a month another skater would indeed do something truly incredible to challenge (and sometimes beat) Tony. The rest of the skaters would quickly copy the winning moves, and Tony would have to dream up something new to stay ahead of the competition. In this way, the entire sport of skateboarding got better.

Got fans?
Tony's huge following has made him a natural for ads aimed at young people.

¿got milk?

The Madonna, Stale Fish, and 720 McHawk. I've named my share of tricks. But my secret weapon came with a name already in place. Milk. It has more nutrients than sports drinks, plus it's one of the few things I don't have to be upside down to enjoy.

got milk?

chapter 5

ups and downs

"I never set a plan for my life. I just rolled with it."
TONY HAWK

At an age when most athletes are just beginning to scratch the surface of their abilities, Tony Hawk was actually pondering retirement. Winning competitions no longer held the thrill it once did, yet when he did not finish first, he felt as if he had finished last. Obviously, he was still a bit of a perfectionist.

Tony liked working on new tricks, but he was growing tired of competing. So in the spring of 1987, instead of joining the NSA tour, Tony accepted another movie role. He played a pizza delivery boy in *Gleaming the Cube*, a film about a young man investigating the murder

Hold that pose.
A fan videotapes Tony at an event in Rhode Island.

of his brother, who was a skateboarder. Stacy Peralta was helping direc-tor Grame Clifford with the skating scenes. Tony got to meet the movie's star, Christian Slater, and had a nice, relaxed time. The movie was released in 1989.

Tony worked on another big project that year: his relationship with Cindy Dunbar. Once a close friend, she had become much closer to Tony, and now they were talking about marriage. First, Tony wanted to buy a new house—one with enough property so he could construct his

own private skatepark. In this custom-built "laboratory" he would work on moves no one had ever dreamed of. And who better to build it than his dad? Frank Hawk showed up at Tony's new home in Fallbrook, California, in January of 1988, and the two began work. By the time they finished, Tony was ready to return to competition.

During Tony's time away from the sport he realized what he liked about it, and what he did *not* like about it. He loved the adrenaline rush of doing a new trick in public for the first time. And he adored the challenge of pushing his sport forward. What Tony did not enjoy was the pressure to win every time. It dawned on him one day that this pressure was coming from one place: himself. Once he understood that his own personality—not the sport itself—was preventing him from having a good time, he knew what to do. He would skate for fun, and the heck with everything else.

check it out...
Tony and Cindy were married in April of 1990. The ceremony was held in their backyard.

Tony came back and had a blast. In 1988 and 1989, he and Cindy traveled the world. They were treated like royalty wherever they went, and Tony skated free and easy. And guess what? He destroyed the competition. Tony was winning *and* having fun—imagine that!

Unfortunately, the fun began to end in 1990. Thanks in large part to Tony, skateboarding had been growing like crazy for several years. But the industry could not maintain its momentum, and sales of equipment began to slump. A lot of companies had jumped on the skateboarding "bandwagon" when things were going well, and now they had no

Yo, I said build a deck!
Just kidding. Tony and his friends try out
the gigantic halfpipe he and his father built in his backyard.

Lord of the board.

Living so close to the Pacific Ocean gave Tony the chance to ride the waves when he was a teenager.

choice but to jump off. Manufacturers began to cancel endorsement deals with the top skaters, and withdraw their support from competitions and exhibitions. With fewer public events, corporate sponsors spent less money on billboards and banners. Although millions of kids still skated, the skateboarding industry itself was "leaking" dollars. Indeed, the entire sport looked like it might crumble.

Tony was hit very hard by this sudden turn of events. His income in 1990 was half

check it out...

In 1988, Tony was hired as a stunt double for David Spade in *Police Academy 4*. He was fired when producers realized he was nearly a foot taller than the comedian.

the hawk file

Tony's favorite . . .

Sport to Watch	Basketball
Athlete to Watch	Lance Armstrong
Actor to Watch	Julianne Moore
Snack	Girl Scout Chocolate Thin Mints
Musical Group	The Pixies
Book	High Fidelity, by Nick Hornby

of what it had been in 1989. In 1991, he made even less. Tony sensed that, as the sport's most revered figure, it was up to him to take a more prominent role. He decided the time was right to start his own company, which he called Birdhouse Projects. Operating on a shoestring budget, he and a former rider for Powell-Peralta named Per Welinder started designing skateboards and building a team along the lines of the old Bones Brigade. "Looking back, I'm stoked skating deep-sixed," Tony says. "It gave me the initiative to start my own company."

Despite Tony's enthusiasm, Birdhouse failed to make money. The skateboard

check it out...

In March of 1992, while Tony was putting on an exhibition in Florida, he got a call from Cindy, who told him that she was pregnant. Later that year she gave birth to Hudson Hawk. He goes by his middle name, Riley.

Chip off the old Hawk.
Young Riley grabs some mad air, just like his dad.

market was still slumping, and Tony was devoting so much time to keeping the business afloat that he was forced to cut back on his competition schedule. That meant even less money coming in. By 1994, Tony had used all of his savings, and Birdhouse was teetering on the edge of bankruptcy. He considered getting a "real" job, but where does a 26-year-old skateboarder go? To help solve their money problems, Tony and Cindy sold their house in Fallbrook and moved into a small place in Irvine. But their marriage was not strong enough to survive this crisis and they eventually decided to get divorced. They agreed to share custody of their two-year-old son, Riley.

TV or not TV.
**That was never the question for Tony. This appearance on Nickelodeon's
All That *was one of many he made during the 1990s.***

Tony's life was a mess. Was he just an overgrown kid who had no business *running* a business? Was fame so fleeting that he was already "washed up" in his mid 20s? Was holding his sport together so important that it was worth losing his family? These questions gnawed at him as he tried to determine his next move.

tricks of the trade

"I don't exactly know how many tricks I've invented," says Tony Hawk. "I'd say anywhere from, like, 70 to 100. Sometimes I have an idea and go to the skatepark and try it out. It may not work, or I look at the ramp and don't even want to try it. But other times, I try something and then, wow! A new trick!" Here are some of Tony's top inventions, along with the year he first did them:

Backside Varial—1980
Airwalk—1983
Stalefish—1985
The 720—1985
Ollie 540—1989
Kickflip McTwist—1994
Frontside Cab Revert—1997
Varial 720—1998
The 900—1999
Stalefish Frontside—2000

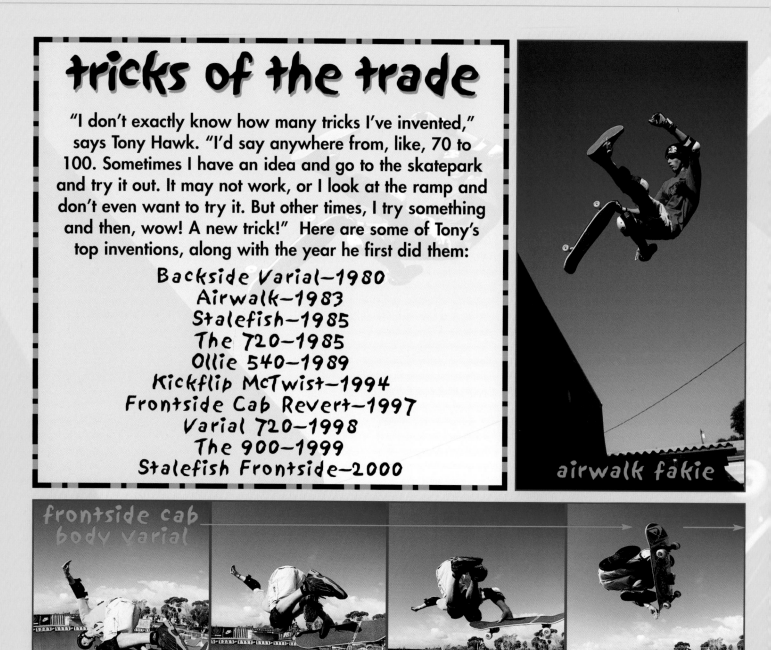

airwalk fakie

frontside cab body varial

taking wing

"Sometimes I can't wait to skate because I don't know what new tricks I'll come up with that day."
TONY HAWK

Tony and Per Welinder put their heads together hoping to find a way to save their floundering business. They devised and then discarded several plans. In time, they came to the realization that there was only one guarantee in skateboarding: If Tony Hawk was skating, a big crowd was going to show up. They reasoned that if Tony hit the pro tour again and

check it out...
Tony does a lot of traveling. When he can't find a luggage cart, he likes to improvise. "You can prop your bag on the front of the board and skate through airports like that," Tony claims.

Back on the block.
Tony's return to touring translated into packed houses at skateboarding events.

dominated as he had in years past, Birdhouse—as well as skateboarding itself—could make a comeback.

On paper, this plan looked good. There was a whole new generation of skaters, and only a handful had seen Tony in action. He would come back strong, show the new guys a thing or two, and then reclaim his throne. However, Tony was afraid his personal life would prevent him from making this commitment. He would not see much of Riley being on the road so often. Also, Frank Hawk was battling cancer. There was

Vinny Vegas · Brian Sumner · Tony Hawk · Willy Santos · Bucky Lasek · Matt Allen · Jeremy Klein · Joey Poiriez · Griffin Collins

birdhouse
SKATEBOARDS

no telling how long he might live, and Tony did not want to be away while his dad's health continued to decline. In short, there did not seem to be an easy answer to Tony's dilemma.

One day late in 1994, Tony finally got some good news. He heard a rumor that ESPN, the round-the-clock sports network, was planning to hold an Olympic-style competition for "extreme sports." It would be called the "X Games" and would include skateboarding. Most of Tony's fellow skaters were worried by this news. They did not trust outsiders who wanted to "showcase" their sport. Tony disagreed. He sensed that this was exactly what it needed. Not only would this reintroduce skateboarding to the world, it would also highlight the great personalities in the sport. When the announcement was officially made, Tony was among the first to tell ESPN he would definitely be there.

That June, millions of young viewers tuned in to see Hawk (at 27, the grand old man of skateboarding) whomp the competition in the "Vert" and come in a close second in the "Street." ESPN's coverage was phenomenal, and it provided an incredible showcase for Tony. He was glad his father got to see all of his runs, but disappointed that the network edited out the performances of other skaters in order to focus on him. Still, the effect on the sport was dramatic. Almost immediately, there was a surge in sales of skateboard equipment. And finally, Tony's company started turning a profit.

Tony hit the road, promoting Birdhouse products and building more interest in the sport. He returned to California to see his family when he could, but business kept him very busy. Then came the call he dreaded: While at Woodward Sports Camp in Pennsylvania, Tony learned his father had passed away. He went home for the funeral and was astounded at the outpouring of love and support from the skateboarding community. Tony had been so wrapped up in his own career that he never really understood what a hero Frank Hawk was to his sport.

The call.
Tony takes a break from the action at Woodward, where he learned that his father had passed away.

Tony felt guilty that he had not been around for his father in his final days. But he knew what Frank would have told him: "Get out there and work!" Tony took this message to heart in 1996, as he approached his business, his career, and his life with renewed vigor. The Birdhouse tour stopped in city after city, attracting thousands of skaters who idolized Tony—and who bought his boards and equipment. In competition, he continued to come up with new tricks. When the 1996 X Games opened in San Francisco, Tony was coming off major wins at the Hard Rock Hotel in Las Vegas and a big meet in Texas. Once again, he was one of ESPN's featured athletes. However, the network honored Tony's request that the focus be less on him and more on skateboarding. Despite a sprained ankle, he finished second in the Street competition. He capped off his run with an unforgettable leap into the Pacific Ocean.

After the X Games, Tony and his girlfriend, Erin, got married. He had been dating her for a couple of years, and his son adored her. Marrying her made total sense. When the newlyweds returned from their honeymoon in Hawaii, Tony began preparing for the 1997 season—another year on the road. Birdhouse was doing well, the sport was on the rise again, and Tony had become a full-fledged media star. There were constant requests for photo shoots and interviews, and his travel schedule was becoming insane. Sometimes he would wake up and not know where he was.

check it out...

Some believe skateboarding might one day be considered as a medal sport by the Olympics. Tony thinks this is a lousy idea—if you put too many rules and regulations on skateboarding, you lose the thing that makes it most fun. "In a competition," he says, "if someone is trying something and time's up, they'll keep going because the crowd wants to see it. There's no way the Olympics would allow for that kind of spontaneity."

taking wing

"Half of
what we do
is just
testing out
what's
possible."
TONY HAWK

Double the fun.
Tony and Andy McDonald took the Vert Doubles at the 1997 X Games.

Tony worried that the demands of stardom might break up his second marriage, and he was not about to make that mistake again. He also knew that the more time he spent attending to the details of his life, the less time he would have to practice. Tony asked his sister Pat to work for him as his manager. She agreed. The man of a hundred moves had just made the smartest move of all.

Free to concentrate on his skating, Tony began to work hard on the 900, a trick no one had ever mastered. The 900 required a skater to power up a ramp, grab some major air, and then complete two-and-a-half turns before skating back down the ramp. Attaining the proper speed was one problem, executing the spins was another, and landing without killing yourself was the final challenge. Some said it could not be done.

The 900 (which gets its name from the "math" involved: $360^\circ + 360^\circ + 180^\circ = 900^\circ$) was called the "Holy Grail" of skateboarding. Tony first got the idea for the 900 when he was 19. It took him another eight years before he began experimenting with it, in 1995. "I tried it off and on," he remembers. "Sometimes I'd get close, sometimes I'd get hurt."

Tony made his first public attempt at the 900 during the 1997 X Games. After two excellent runs in the Vert competition, he knew he had clinched first place. So on his third run, he built up a head of steam and launched himself in the air. The first two spins were smooth, but the last half-spin came too late. Tony ended up in a pile at the bottom of the ramp. The crowd cheered loudly as he smiled and dragged himself away. Later, Tony teamed with Andy McDonald and won the Vert Doubles, a new competition.

As the 1997 season drew to a close, Tony had to feel good about his life. He had weathered personal and professional storms, and was now just where he wanted to be. Among his goals for 1998 was to shoot a Birdhouse video in the tradition of Stacy Peralta's old Bones Brigade tapes. He spent $100,000 producing *The End,* which debuted in the fall. It quickly became the top-selling video in the sport. Tony also started work on a line of skate-inspired clothing. It, too, was a smashing success. In competition, Tony enjoyed one of his best years. He won nine events, and defended his crown in the Vert Doubles at the 1998 X Games.

The only thing that eluded Tony was the 900.

tick-tock...tick-tock...

1976
Gets first skateboard from brother

1980
California Amateur Skateboard League formed by Tony's dad

1981
Joins Bones Brigade at age 13

1986
Graduates from high school & stars in Mountain Dew commercial

1985
Appears in FUTURE PRIMITIVE video

1983
National Skateboarding Association formed by Tony's dad

basic stuff

Home	San Diego, CA
Born	May 12, 1968 Carlsbad, CA
Height	6' 2" (188 cm)
Weight	170 lbs (77 kg)

timeline

1998
Produces first video, The End

1999
Lands history's first 900

1997
Gets his own
SI for Kids trading card

1995
Stars in first
X Games

1992
Starts Birdhouse Projects

2001
Releases Pro Skater 3

1987
Plays a pizza boy in
GLEAMING THE CUBE (released in 1989)

TONY HAWK

SKATEBOARDER
CARLSBAD, CALIFORNIA

Sports Illustrated
KIDS

 chapter 7

 soaring

"He's like a role model to us."
PRO SKATEBOARDER BOB BURNQUIST

By the end of 1998, Tony Hawk was bigger than he (or anyone else) ever imagined a skater could be. The sport was hot, his company was hot, and he was the person the whole world pictured when they heard the word "skateboard." Tony was so popular that Pat was getting overwhelmed. She suggested that he hire an agent. Tony settled on the William Morris Agency, a California firm that represented some of the world's most famous celebrities.

Generation next.
Skaters who grew up idolizing Tony, like Bob Burnquist, now appear on their own trading cards.

Bob Burnquist
Skateboarder • Vista, California

Fence busters.
Tony hates to put barriers between himself and his fans, but sometimes it's a matter of self-preservation.

Tony's fellow skateboarders reacted negatively to this decision. One of the things they liked about their sport was that it had resisted the hype and phoniness of other sports. Some said Tony had "sold out," that he was putting himself above skateboarding to make more money. Many fans felt the same way. In the skateboarding magazine *Big Brother*, he was voted the "most hated" skater. Not *everyone* agreed. In the same magazine poll, Tony was voted second in the "most liked" skater category! "There is always the accusation that I've sold out," Tony acknowledges. "But ever since I was 14, I've had skateboard products with my name attached. The only difference now is that they actually sell."

Looking back, it is obvious that everyone missed the point. What Tony was doing was exploring uncharted territory, and that made some people nervous. No one in skateboarding had ever gained this much recognition, and Tony realized he had a chance to do something special for his sport. In order to make good things happen, however, he now had to be extra-careful about the opportunities that were coming his way. Tony remembered

check it out...

Tony thinks it is time for others in his sport to consider hiring agents. "Skaters don't know their worth outside of the skateboard world, and, at least right now, we need people on our side to tell us what that worth is."

Gone ape.
***Tony got rave reviews from his younger fans after they saw his moves in the animated Disney film* Tarzan.**

how naive some of his decisions were back in the 1980s, and did not want to repeat his mistakes. Only an experienced, professional business representative could help him make intelligent choices. At the same time, Tony knew that his days as a competitive skater might be numbered—he needed to think about the future. He was in his 30s, and although his body was still supple, the aches and pains of skating lingered more with each passing year. Tony quietly decided that 1999 would be his final season as a full-time competitor.

That was about the only quiet thing in Tony's life. In March, he and Erin had a son, Spencer. Tony and his agents had a ton of offers to sort through. He also began to rub elbows with some of Hollywood's biggest celebrities—many of whom had children who idolized him. When the Disney movie *Tarzan* premiered, Tony was at the opening. The movie's creators had used many of the moves from *The End* in the animated film's action scenes. Then there was the video game—Tony Hawk's Pro Skater—which he agreed to help design. And on top of everything, he was now skateboarding's unofficial "goodwill ambassador." Wherever Tony went, he was expected to shake hands, sign autographs, and turn people on to his sport.

In between his business commitments, Tony entered a handful of contests and exhibitions. His goal was to get himself in peak form for the 1999 X Games. By the time he reached San Francisco, he was ready to blow everyone away. After placing third in the Vert, Tony readied himself for the new "Best Trick" competition.

Tony positioned himself on the edge of the ramp and took a slow, deep breath. He was as focused and determined as anyone had ever seen him. It had been two years since he had tried and failed to pull off the 900. Now it was dawning on the crowd—one of the largest ever to witness a skateboarding event—what was about to happen. Tony was going for the 900 again. "I was either landing that trick or waking up in the hospital," Tony admits.

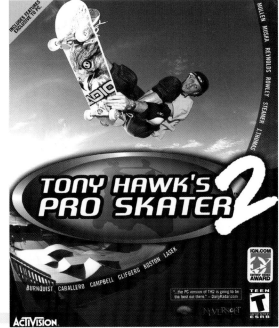

Tony's fellow skaters bristled with excitement. They began banging their boards on the ground, to get him psyched up. Moments later, Tony Hawk was airborne. He twisted once, then twice, then a half-time more. He hit the ramp hard on his return, but kept his balance. The 900 was

Game face.
Tony has already moved on to Pro Skater 3. The series is now one of the best-selling games of all time.

Miss you much.

There is one person missing from the crowds that come out to see Tony's exhibitions: his dad.

in the books. It had been done. "Everyone went completely mental," one fellow skater recalled.

Tony cracked a wide smile as he was mobbed by the other competitors. He stepped up to the microphone and hollered, "This is the best day of my life! I couldn't have done it without you! This is the best moment of all time!"

After pulling off his 900 at the X Games, Tony thought it would be cool to retire, to leave his sport on top. However, he had already promised to compete in other events, and did not want to let the promoters down. Tony went out in style later in the year, winning his last event at the Vans Triple Crown. He only had one regret. "It's hard to believe that so many people around the world saw me land that '9,' and the one person who would have appreciated it the most wasn't there," Tony says. "Out of all my skateboarding accomplishments, I wish my dad was still alive to have seen me do it."

> "I'm pretty happy with the way things turned out.
> I mean, I never thought that I could make a career
> out of skateboarding."
> TONY HAWK

Although Tony no longer competes ("I just do exhibition-style skating now"), he is on his board almost every day. That may never change. However, many things *have* changed. The wave of popularity that followed his 900 almost swept his family away. People were ringing his doorbell day and night hoping to meet him and get his autograph. This got very annoying (and a little scary) so he moved to a more secure house with a gate in front. Tony knows that it looks like he is separating himself from his fans, but he had no choice.

Retirement gave Tony more time to devote to his business, which also took off. The Pro Skater video game sold more than two million copies, and new versions were gobbled up by his fans the second they hit the stores. Hawk Clothing was doing so well that Tony was able to make a deal that brought his designs to malls all over the country.

Father time.
Now Tony is the dad watching his son (Riley) roll up the ramps.

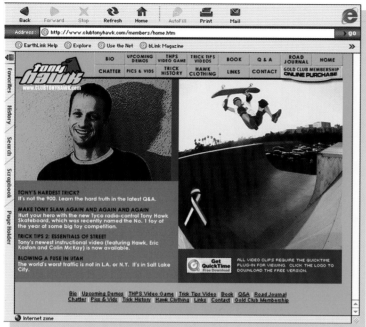

Tony's newest ventures include a movie production company called 900 Films, and his own fan-club Web site, www.club-tonyhawk.com. He also agreed to be a commentator at the X Games, and serve as an online reporter for EXPN.com.

What's the coolest thing about being Tony Hawk? According to Tony, it is watching Riley and Spencer master the art of skateboarding. He claims that both have his talent for the sport—and he now admits that he appreciates how worried his parents must have been when he first started skating. "It makes me proud that I can switch from being a skater to a responsible parent," Tony says.

"But I don't feel as old as other parents," he quickly adds.

Indeed, there is still plenty of teenager left in Tony. Just listen to him give advice to his boys. When they ask if it's okay to try something new (and even when they don't), his philosophy is the same now as it was when he was their age. "If you want to try something new," Tony smiles, "go for it!"

Roll model.
Tony has inspired yet another generation of young skateboarders.
He thinks one of these kids—maybe Shaun White—could be the first to do a 1080.

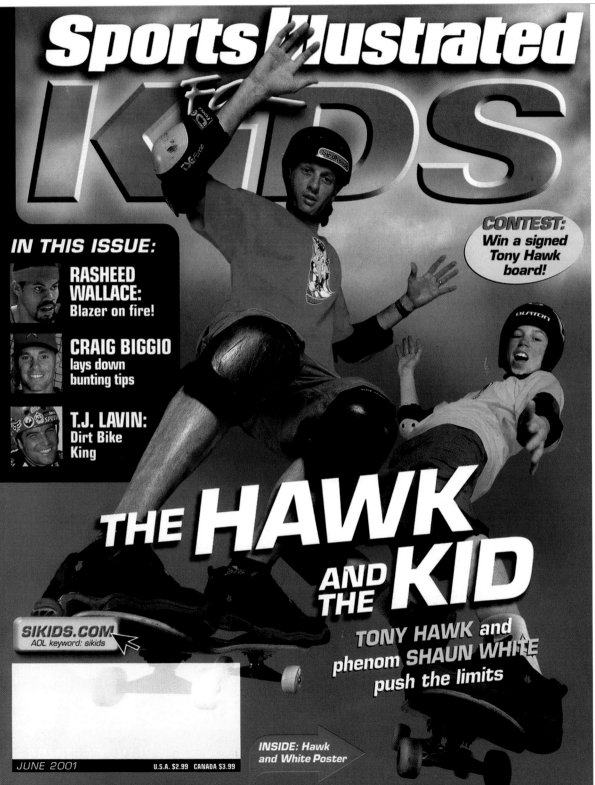

Sports Illustrated KIDS

CONTEST:
Win a signed
Tony Hawk
board!

IN THIS ISSUE:

RASHEED WALLACE:
Blazer on fire!

CRAIG BIGGIO
lays down
bunting tips

T.J. LAVIN:
Dirt Bike
King

THE HAWK AND THE KID

TONY HAWK and
phenom SHAUN WHITE
push the limits

SIKIDS.COM
AOL keyword: sikids

JUNE 2001   U.S.A. $2.99   CANADA $3.99

INSIDE: Hawk
and White Poster

Mr. 900

Tony Hawk's remarkable 900 was replayed again and again on television, and his photo appeared in magazines and newspapers around the globe. As a result, he became one of the most recognized figures in sports. Indeed, many people who have never set foot on a skateboard

can now pick him out of a crowd. This makes the simple things Tony took for granted—like shopping and dining—almost impossible to do now. When he steps out of his car, it becomes a public event. And wherever he goes a trail of kids forms behind him. "Sometimes it's weird to be out doing normal things and trying to get something done when people recognize you and want some of your time," he says. "It's an honor to be recognized like that, but it's also hard."

what's that called again?

Board Basics

DECK
The part of the skateboard you stand on

KICKTAIL
The back end of the skateboard

NOSE
The front end of the skateboard

TRUCKS
The swiveling connectors between the skateboard's axles and deck

Popular Stunts

AIRWALK
Rider keeps one foot on board and one in air

FAKIE
Rider rolls backward but continues to look forward

KICKFLIP
Rider spins board with foot

OLLIE
Rider and board elevate off the ground together

VARIAL
Rider turns board in midair

720
Rider completes two turns in the air

900
Rider completes two-and-a-half turns in the air

where do you get this stuff?

For more information on skateboarding, check out these resources!

Skateboarding Magazines...

Skateboarder
Thrasher
Big Brother
Transworld Skateboarding
Heckler

General Sports Magazines...

Sports Illustrated for Kids
ESPN the Magazine

Skateboarding Books...

The Concrete Wave, *Michael Brooke*
Skateboarding: To the Extreme, *Bill Gutman*
The Ultimate Skateboard Book, *Albert Cassorla*
Skateboarding, *Mike Kennedy*

Skateboarding Web Sites...

United Skateboarding Association (unitedskate.com)
World Cup Skateboarding (wcs8.com)
The Skateboard Link (skateboardlink.com)

index